CULTIVATING THE SOCIOME:

GOVERNANCE WITHOUT GOVERNORS

ERIC MOON

First Printing, 2025
Cover Design: David Ryan

ISBN (Paperback): 979-8-9853348-5-2
IBSN (Ebook): 979-8-9853348-6-9

Respect Nature's Wisdom

CONTENTS

PREFACE

This book stems from a podcast series that I produced beginning in 2021, called *Fascinating!*

The term "fascinating," of course, derives from the Star Trek universe; it was Spock's go-to comment in response to things humans said and did that he, as an ultra-rational being, found inexplicable.

In the podcast, I assumed the persona of Rik from Planet Vulcan, and my initial mission on Planet Earth was to search for signs of intelligence and to encourage its spread, for the purpose of contributing to the development of Earth's societies.

I used the "Vulcan's-eye view" as a device to show, first of all, that my chosen perspective on issues of political economy did not include allegiance to any faction or party on Planet Earth, nor did it concern itself with current hot-button issues—what I referred to as "arranging the deck chairs," and also compared it to the mock battle between Tweedledee and Tweedledum in the Dark Woods.

Instead, the podcast essays were more concerned with fundamental thinking about larger issues—the nature of reality and the nature of human existence and human society—a way of thinking that can be of value to all of us, regardless of who we are or what agendas we might be committed to.

At the same time that I was trying to help educate listeners about *good* thinking, I also drew attention to examples of what I believed was "ecnarongi," ignorance spelled backwards, which is "knowin' so durn much that ain't so," in the words attributed to Mark Twain and echoed by George Bernard Shaw, Frank Knight, and other notables. Their message was that "it ain't ignorance that's the problem."

Later in the series, I modified my mission statement to one of planting seeds of a way of thinking built on an understanding of evolutionary processes, with the aim of helping Earthlings move on from the pre-Darwinian intelligent-design modes of thought that we have inherited from medieval times, and which have long dominated—and still dominate—in many areas outside the serious study of the natural sciences. This includes popular thinking about biological evolution, of course, but also popular thinking about institutions and governance, and much academic thinking about these issues as well.

It seemed apparent to me that most people's belief systems were missing something vital: they had not yet accommodated the insight revealed in the work of Charles Darwin and other naturalists—namely, the understanding that many natural phenomena that appear to be the product of design can be plausibly, even convincingly, explained as having arisen spontaneously, without a designer.

I hoped that achieving an understanding of the natural phenomenon of spontaneous emergent order would lead to the abandonment of belief in, and support for, policies and institutions rooted in a belief in intelligent design.

A belief in intelligent design typically leads to the conclusion that getting us all on the path to a better future depends on wresting control from an imaginary class of designers and rulers motivated by evil intentions, and putting control into the hands of designers who are more nobly motivated—men with "compassion and vision," in the words of the Steely Dan song. We could depend on these leaders, we imagined, to make things "turn out right," like the *deus ex machina* in plays by Euripides and other ancient Greek dramatists.

The major problem with this intelligent-design approach is that the only evidence for the very *existence* of such a class of rulers is the observed fact of order in the world we live in, peppered with a few anecdotes, and the belief that the existence of order *presupposes* that there is some agent doing the designing and giving the orders.

We will not find many examples of circular reasoning that are more clear-cut than this one.

But if we understand the idea of emergent order, we see that there is no convincing reason to believe in the very existence of a ruling class without further evidence besides the observation of order—and I don't mean anecdotes and conspiratorial dot-connecting.

For most of my adult life, I lived in the San Francisco Bay Area. Very few among my friends and acquaintances had *not* signed on to the notion that the path to a better future was to oust the people with bad intentions and to put people with good intentions into positions of authority, and then to provide them with huge budgets and instructions to "make it so."

My circle of friends and acquaintances—all of them kind and amiable companions—were uniformly convinced of the virtue of their political leanings, mostly on account of the good intentions on which those leanings were founded. They did not want to listen to any evidence that the actual consequences of their well-intended policies have been, and continue to be, suboptimal at best—for reasons that are well understood—and which often add up to a significant net minus for global well-being, in spite of the good intentions that motivated them.

I don't believe that good intentions combined with the exercise of authority is likely to be a recipe for good outcomes, even when leaders sincerely try, because events have a life of their own, and reality is disinclined to be obedient.

Deus ex machina may be the intention of the interventions, but *diabolus ex machina* is more often than not the real-world result.

It slowly dawned on me that I was swimming in a sea that was more akin to a religious movement than to a genuine scientific pursuit of knowledge and understanding. So I resolved to mostly just enjoy the company of these dear friends while realizing that trying to talk to them about economics, my area of expertise, was very little different from trying to talk to a committed fundamentalist Christian about evolution.

Few adults over the age of thirty ever change their minds about anything, so among this older cohort I expected my message would continue to fall on deaf ears.

But I reasoned that it still might be a fruitful endeavor to direct an educational message toward younger people, and others who are still working at achieving a worldview based on the scientific investigation of nature, and who might still be open to approaches that lie outside the conventional wisdom and outside the institutions we have inherited from medieval Europe.

I reasoned that knowledge of the fundamental notion of the spontaneous order that arises from a social dynamic—in which most of us, most of the time, observe a simple set of rules that we apply only locally—would allow us to move past the pre-Darwinian medievalist thinking that still dominates in today's world.

That pre-Darwinian thinking dominates is true particularly among those who study the social sciences and humanities, but also true of many who study the natural sciences but who nonetheless subscribe to medievalist thinking when they think and talk about politics and human society.

Many of these scientists seem unaware of the contradiction between their approach to understanding natural science and their approach to understanding human society, and those who are aware of the contradiction are reluctant to speak up and then undergo the vilification and ostracism that is the fate of heretics, and to which I can personally testify. So happy that the practice of burning at the stake has been suspended for now.

My hope is that once a critical mass of people forms whose beliefs are informed by the lessons from science and nature that lead to an understanding of spontaneous self-organization, we can progress from the currently popular idea that we have the ability to collectively design and structure our socioeconomic system, to the idea that our socioeconomic system is actually an evolving sociome with a life of its own, and not at all analogous to a static structure that we can build. Our efforts would then be more profitably directed toward cultivating the sociome with a focus on process rather than on structure, and letting the structures take care of themselves.

I believe there is a strong impetus toward a wider understanding of the consequences of evolutionary thinking among people who are still forming a worldview and are interested in grounding their worldview in a scientific study of nature.

We can expect progress in this direction to be slow, as those among us who are set in our ways cling with tenacity to outmoded institutions, and especially to their roles within these institutions.

As the eminent physicist Max Planck phrased it, scientific progress occurs one funeral at a time. And it's the polite thing to do to wait for them to die.

INTRODUCTION

Towards the end of his life, the eminent biologist Edward O. Wilson, in a magazine interview where he was discussing his views on the meaning of life, made this statement:

"The real problem of humanity is the following: we have Paleolithic emotions, medieval institutions, and godlike technology."

I don't have much in the way of suggestions about how to deal with the Paleolithic emotions or the godlike technology. I do, however, have at least one suggestion about how to move beyond our medieval institutions.

The suggestion is this: we can replace the old paradigm based on what I call intelligent design with a new paradigm that is based on an understanding of natural evolution and the way of nature.

If the implications of this proposed paradigm are unclear to you, you are not to blame, and you are by no means alone. Our systems of educating the young so far include very little in the way of evolutionary thinking and the principles of self-organization.

I believe it is, however, vitally important for us all to see clearly what the implications of the old and new paradigms are if we want our cultural evolution to take us and our progeny in the direction of happy and prosperous societies characterized by less conflict than what we now experience.

Here is an attempt at characterizing the old and new paradigms:

An intelligent design paradigm rests on the idea that a group of rulers must exercise oversight and regulation of individual and institutional behavior so as to control real-world outcomes, with the aim of trying to make those outcomes conform as closely as possible to some ideal.

Conflict is frequently the result of a contest for who it is that gets to exercise the power, and for that reason among other reasons no one seems to get around to doing much more than trying to gain power.

An evolutionary paradigm, on the other hand, rests on the idea that outcomes are fundamentally beyond our control, due to the complexity that exists both in ourselves and in the real world, and that what we can in truth directly affect by choice does not extend beyond our choice of means. We will never be able to choose ends and then create the means that will take us to those ends.

Thanks to the legendary Buckminster Fuller for his insight that systems are organized by the energy flowing through them - an idea that helps us understand that as we choose the means and try to implement them, what we end up doing is to add to the energy flows within the system. These energy flows then result *de facto* in the organization of the overall system, even if we believe that what we are doing is choosing ends.

Social animals, including humans, create a kind of orderly organization by observing simple sets of rules, rules that each creature applies only locally, and the observance of which leads spontaneously to the emergence of large-scale order.

For example, fish, grazing mammals, and birds instinctively behave in ways that lead to the emergence of the superorganisms we call schools, herds, and flocks. And social insects such as ants and bees instinctively behave in ways that lead to the emergence of the superorganisms we call anthills and beehives.

Governance without governors.

Likewise, the emergence of order in the human sociome will always and forever depend on the set of rules we as individuals generally follow and apply in our respective localities. We must be mindful of the fact that although we humans do have some instinctive behavior, we also have behavior that arises from the use of our spectacularly complex brains. Unlike ants and bees, we can to some extent pick and choose among the rules we will actually follow.

If you find the ideas expressed in the previous paragraphs new and puzzling, you are currently in the majority. Spontaneous emergent order is a fairly new idea and one that is only just beginning to find its place in our collective consciousness.

We humans too can have governance without governors, just like the birds and the bees. And in truth, we already have much governance that takes place without governors, even if we do not recognize it as such. If you are skeptical that such a thing as governance without governors could actually work, I tell you it is already working—and on a massive scale.

Those among us who have not previously been exposed to the idea of order without orders find it difficult to believe and are often surprised when they first hear about the spontaneous emergence of order in the natural world. They are even more surprised when they hear about the spontaneous emergence of order in human society.

Our conventional wisdom consists of carryovers from olden times. We have inherited a worldview based on the ways of medieval thought, institutions, and social organization, where kings ruled by divine right and where rule-making, oversight, and control of the lower classes were the province of the inhabitants of the castles, the churches, and the manor houses. Most people believed, and many still do, that without this sort of regimentation imposed from above - or at least strong leadership - the achievement of order would be impossible.

But in the towns, outside the jurisdiction of the castles and the manor houses, practices of production and commerce evolved in a way that demonstrated there can indeed be order without anyone intentionally "making it so." And an even bigger surprise was that the order that was generated spontaneously led to far greater efficiency and general well-being than the order that had been imposed from the castles.

So read on. In this book I have distilled the ideas contained in my podcast essays and have tried to put them all together in an accessible form. If you read carefully, you can catch on to the proposed new paradigm of evolutionary thinking, and as this modern paradigm spreads, we can lay the intelligent design paradigm to rest—or at least push it to the sidelines—with salutary results for humanity.

1

EMERGENCE AND EMERGENT ORDER

The concept of emergent order as a generally applicable paradigm is rooted in the work of the English barnacle specialist Charles Darwin and his contemporary, the brilliant self-taught naturalist Alfred Russel Wallace. They were the first to demonstrate in modern times that something that looks like design in nature can arise without a designer.

As a famous example of this, Darwin showed that the finches on the Galápagos Islands *appeared* to have been designed to match their respective food sources: some had large, powerful beaks for cracking tough seeds; some had long, slender beaks for probing tree bark or cactus flowers; and some had sharp, pointed beaks suited for preying on insects.

All of the finches had presumably descended from a common ancestor, but over time they had become distinct species, each with a beak that looked finely engineered, yet had actually arisen through a blind, cumulative process.

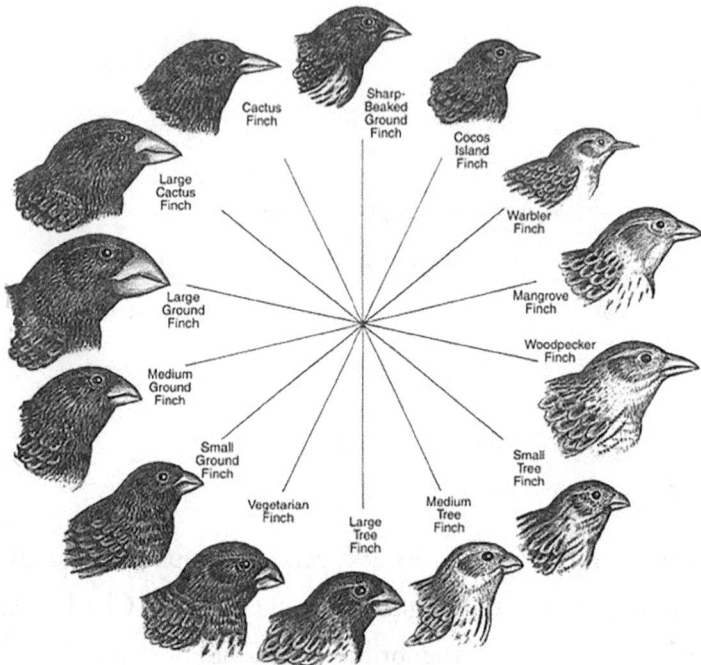

Darwin also pointed to the selective breeding of pigeons to illustrate his idea. He noted that *intentional* selection by humans - choosing which birds would mate - could demonstrably produce striking changes in a short time. Darwin's leap was to show that *unintentional* selection, operating over vast spans of time, could explain what looks like design not only in pigeons but in all living things.

It quickly dawned on some that this revelation—that the existence of order does not prove the presence of an intelligent designer—would eventually lead to a drastic reordering of human thought in many other areas as well.

Emergence as a general concept is a fairly recent and quite exciting topic in the study of science and nature. Until recently, scientists understood their task primarily in reductionist terms rather than in terms of emergence.

A reductionist approach explains a phenomenon as the sum of its parts. For example, we explain heat as the energetic motion of molecules.

Examples of emergent phenomena include the intelligence present in an animal's brain, even though the individual neurons are not intelligent at all; the seemingly intelligent behavior of an insect colony, even though the individual bugs are not themselves intelligent; and the rational outcomes that are achieved in market economies, even though individual human market participants do not necessarily behave rationally.

In his book *Darwin's Dangerous Idea*, the late Tufts University philosopher Daniel Dennett argued that whatever else might happen to Darwin's theory of evolution by natural selection, one novel idea will certainly persist: what looks like design can occur without any designer. In other words, order in nature emerges spontaneously.

The significance of this idea is that it dismantles the myths and common beliefs that the existence of order can only be explained as the work of an intelligent designer, as well as an intelligent overseer.

Followers of theistic religions often dismiss the notion of emergence and emergent order simply because they are highly motivated to cling to the idea of a creator who has promised them eternal life in paradise. It is not easy, once having believed this promise, to accept one's mortality.

Non-theists, meanwhile, may dismiss emergence for other reasons. Many simply cannot imagine alternatives to the medieval institutions we are still saddled with, cannot envision how things could actually work if we gave them up, and mistake their failure of imagination for proof that no alternatives exist.

Dennett used the metaphor of a "universal acid" for Darwin's dangerous idea—because a universal acid eats through anything it touches, even a container meant to hold it.

I can already hear some responses: "Well, I get the idea of spontaneous order, but it only applies to nature. Humans are different from animals, so we can opt out of the natural order and create our own."

My purpose in this book is to convince you that we humans have no such option. We are as much a part of nature as anything else and are subject to the constraints nature imposes. The universal acid eats right through this attempt at containment.

And I hope to convince you further that this awareness is not cause for despair but a reason for hope. Understanding how things actually work in the natural world—not just around us but as part of us—opens possibilities for improving human well-being that give us realistic justification for hope.

This awareness also helps explain the futility of many past and present attempts to improve society that are grounded in the intelligent-design paradigm, such as national economic planning or pervasive intervention and regulation.

So let's talk about those new possibilities.

The traditional intelligent-design method for improving human well-being begins with imagining a structural model of society as the desired end. For example, many of us gravitate toward the idea that the ideal society is egalitarian, or toward the idea that the ideal society is one where risk has been eliminated.

Once we have chosen our ideal structure, we attempt to create the means to bring it about from what we imagine is our lofty perch above the fray. These means typically involve employing the institution of government to impose requirements and prohibitions on individual actions, enforced socially or legally, and to gain the authority to tax and spend.

The evolutionary method, by contrast, begins with the understanding that nature does not allow us to start with chosen ends and then force them into being. In practice, we can only choose means, and those means produce extremely complex adaptive processes and ways of functioning that create ever-changing structures—structures that cannot be predicted or controlled. This remains true even when we believe we are choosing ends rather than means.

No one stated this more succinctly than the American civil rights leader Martin Luther King, who wrote, "The end is preexistent in the means; the end is the result of the means, just as the tree is contained in the seed."

New vistas open when we recognize that we have a realistic alternative to focusing on societal structure—and that alternative is to focus on societal processes.

Structures are always temporary in any case. Even in the unlikely event that we were to succeed in building the ideal structure we had imagined, events would soon sweep it away. We need to focus on process and get comfortable with the fact that outcomes will always take care of themselves.

And no one is truly above the fray, except in imagination. We are all just cells in a superorganism—the sociome. We, the present set of individuals, constitute that superorganism for a relatively brief span of time. A hundred years from now, it will still be the same superorganism, but most of us will probably have been replaced by other individuals.

It seems inevitable that evolutionary thinking will eventually replace, or at least come to dominate, intelligent-design thinking as the general human mode of thought—despite widespread ignorance so far, and despite attempts to contain it by those who, for whatever reason, are reluctant to release their grip on the reins.

Let's take a brief look at some natural phenomena where macro-organization emerges from micro-level interactions.

Consider the order we observe in nonliving systems: rivers and their tributaries, snowflakes, clouds, sand dunes.

The order we observe in sand dunes, for example, is ultimately the result of the wind blowing the grains of sand, and the grains of various sizes encountering random obstacles, all of which results in a field of dunes of various sizes distributed roughly in accordance with what physicists term a power law.

Consider the order in living systems: slime molds, schools of fish, flocks of birds, insect colonies, packs of predators, and herds of grazing mammals.

Traditional explanations ascribed the order in living systems to top-down control: the queen bee was thought to be the boss of the hive; schools of fish, flocks of birds, and herds of mammals were thought to follow a leader; wolf packs were thought to follow the alpha male.

Think of the 2015 movie *Ant-Man*, where ants are portrayed as individually intelligent creatures that work in teams under a leader. An entertaining story, perhaps, but only if you overlook the bad science—not just the comic-book physics of resizing battle tanks without worrying about conservation of mass, but especially the idea that ant colonies operate under centralized leadership. In reality, the intelligent-seeming behavior of ants emerges only at the level of the colony. Individual ants are automatons whose behavior is entirely instinctive and not at all intelligent.

Evolutionary thinking has overturned traditional explanations by showing that living systems do not, in truth, have bosses or leaders or choreographers. Order arises instead from the behavior of the smallest components of the system, following simple local rules, and from this small-scale behavior, large-scale order emerges spontaneously.

Ants, for example, have evolved responses to touch and taste that result in effective foraging, nest building, reproduction, and defense. No individual ant knows or cares about the colony's organization and seemingly purposeful behavior, yet nature has sculpted their behaviors in such a way that organization emerges on the macro scale.

Flocks of birds, schools of fish, and herds of mammals follow simple rules of individual behavior. Nature has selected for individuals who obey the rules that generate group-level order, to the benefit of the members as well as the group—even though no individual can or does have the group organization in mind or any conception of what behavior will benefit the group.

Researchers have shown that birds in a flock respond only to the behavior of about half a dozen nearby birds. They react in about a tenth of a second, keeping the flock in formation despite disturbances, even though no single bird is aware of the larger patterns that are such a delight for us to observe.

And then there is slime mold, or *Physarum*—perhaps the most astonishing example of emergent order in the natural world.

Physarum is an agglomeration of single-celled organisms that resemble amoebas. It has numerous nuclei but no interior cell membranes, no nervous system, and no musculature. Yet it exhibits behavior that seems intelligent.

Researchers have found that *Physarum* can sense mechanical cues in its environment and make decisions on growth direction based on what it senses. It uses its outer membranes to detect slight deformations, called strain patterns, in substrates, and it prefers smoother substrates over rougher ones.

Physarum forms smart networks by dynamically and continuously adjusting its tubular network in response to environmental changes. The contractile tubes respond to both mechanical and chemical signals. This enables the organism to effectively process information about its immediate environs and produce well-informed behaviors.

Physarum can learn from experience and retain memories, despite not having a conventional nervous system. For example, researchers have observed that if it repeatedly encounters a harmless irritant, it will habituate and reduce its avoidance behavior.

When it is environmentally stressed—too cold, too dry, or too hungry—it will form fruiting bodies. Specific genes activate in response to the chemical signals that the stress creates, and this triggers a cascade of molecular events that ultimately lead to spore production.

Nature has selected for behavior where it is as if the organism is thinking, "I am in mortal danger and might very well perish, so just in case I do die, I will ensure that new organisms will develop from my spores and then agglomerate into the usual superorganism."

Physarum can also perform what amount to sophisticated mathematical calculations.

There is a much-studied problem in network optimization called the "Traveling Salesman Problem," stated thusly: "Given a list of cities and the distances between each pair of cities, what is the shortest possible route that visits each city exactly once and returns to the starting city?"

Solving this problem algorithmically has proven, so far, to be intractable, particularly as the number of cities becomes large, because the possible combinations of routes increase factorially with the number of cities. Brute-force computing has not so far been successful at solving the Traveling Salesman Problem (TSP) beyond dealing with a small number of cities.

The factorial of a number (written $x!$) is equal to the number x itself multiplied by all of the positive integers that precede it. If something is increasing factorially, the results get very large very quickly. For example, the factorial of 5 equals 120; the factorial of 10 equals 3,628,800; the factorial of 20 equals 2,432,903,008,176,640,000. By the time you get to the factorial of 50, you are approaching the number of atoms in the observable universe.

We should not be surprised, therefore, that brute-force computing cannot solve the TSP. But *Physarum* routinely—and quickly—creates networks among food sources that approach optimality, without necessarily arriving at the ultimate solution.

It accomplishes its foraging by exploring randomly at first, sending out pseudopods (tubes) in many directions. As nutrients are found, protoplasmic flow increases in the tubes leading to food. Tubes that carry more flow become thicker (reinforced), while underused tubes shrink and disappear.

Over time, this feedback loop produces an efficient network connecting food sources—often very close to the mathematically optimal network (e.g., the shortest or least-cost path).

Achieving optimality in a network solution is analogous to achieving profit maximization in the world of markets. Just as *Physarum* seeks to maximize the difference between energy expenditure and nutrient value, a business enterprise seeks to maximize the difference between the cost of production and the market value of output.

In both cases, maximization is usually not perfectly attained, but an approximation is usually sufficient. Economists call it "satisficing."

It is important to note here that, in the case of a business enterprise as well as in the case of *Physarum*, satisficing is the result of selection pressure and not the result of rational calculation.

And in both cases, successful operation depends on complex, evolved feedback loops. Remember that the next time you hear someone with plans for intervention in the economy—based on some grand design or other—recklessly proposing to interfere with the emergent prices and the evolved feedback loops on which the functioning of the system depends.

Social insects such as bees, ants, and termites also effectively solve network problems related to their foraging activities, and in much the same way as *Physarum*.

There are also some evolved cultural phenomena in human society that demonstrate emergent order as a result of individuals following a simple set of rules.

We have, for example, the organization of automobile traffic which, all kidding aside, really should impress us with how effective it is. And it all works because most of us, most of the time, voluntarily follow a simple set of rules that assign right-of-way.

Markets provide another example. Markets work effectively and efficiently because most of us, most of the time, respect property rights and contracts, and because prices provide individuals with the information needed to make rational choices. By comparing personal subjective valuations with market prices, individuals decide whether something is worth the cost. Collectively, this produces remarkably well-organized market activity most of the time, and not the chaos that adherents of intelligent-design thinking believe will emerge in the absence of a visible guiding hand.

And it's important to understand that "value" is a broad concept, extending beyond financial value to encompass everything subject to human preference and choice.

It should now be clear that traditional intelligent-design thinking is far less effective and useful than evolutionary thinking.

Yet traditional thinkers remain—many of them not merely unmoved by the power of evolutionary thought processes, but actively resisting its spread, hubristically believing that they can produce results that are superior to the results produced by evolutionary processes.

Why has acceptance been so slow, even among the aware? The reasons may be unimportant in the long run. There have always been those with a vested interest in the established order. Outdated thinking rarely disappears because old thinkers change their minds; it disappears because old thinkers are replaced by new thinkers.

I believe strongly in the universal acid metaphor: attempts to contain evolutionary thinking are ultimately doomed. As Professor Dennett put it, the universal acid eats through every container. Those of us spreading the word about evolutionary thinking hope only to hasten this process.

The next chapters will explore some basic ideas relevant to understanding the sociome and its functioning.

2

LESSONS FROM SOCIOBIOLOGY

The science of sociobiology is the investigation of the influence of genetic evolution on the behavior of social creatures, such as insects and social vertebrates, including humans. The originator of the term, Edward O. Wilson, subtitled his 1975 book on the subject "The New Synthesis", in recognition of the concept's far-reaching implications.

To explain how sociobiologists approach the question of social behavior in general, let's use an analogy.

Many of you are familiar with the Necker cube. The Necker cube is a two-dimensional representation of a three-dimensional object, the cube, but a representation that gives no guidance to the viewer about how to perceive depth. We the viewers can imagine two different axes along which the depth might run and two different faces that might represent the front face. If we stare at one of these pictures we can make our perceptions of depth flip; or our perceptions might flip even if we don't try.

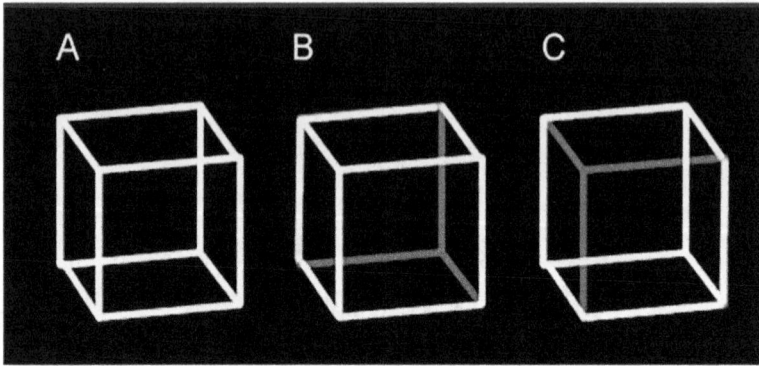

The Necker cube can be a metaphor for the different ways in which we might interpret biological evolution, and points our thinking in the direction of an alternate point of view.

For example, is the egg the chicken's way of making another chicken, or is the chicken the egg's way of making another egg?

We're accustomed to thinking of the egg as the chicken's way of making another chicken, and there's nothing wrong with that; but it's not the only way of thinking about it, and there is no right way.

By choosing, alternatively, to look at the question from the point of view of the egg, scientists have developed deep and important insights into the processes of evolution, because selection occurs primarily at the level of the gene, which dwells within the egg. This focus has led not only to the study of anatomy and physiology with deeper understanding but also to the study of social behavior.

We can view the chicken as a sort of robot that has been designed by its genes to behave in such a way that it will produce more eggs.

Sociobiologists have also refined the concept of fitness and introduced the concept of "inclusive fitness." The old phrase "survival of the fittest," first coined by Herbert Spencer and then adopted by

Charles Darwin, although it was suggestive, previously meant little more than "survival of the survivors," and provided only limited insight into how natural selection works.

Now scientists define fitness rigorously, namely as success in getting copies of one's genes into future generations. "Inclusive fitness" extends the concept of fitness to getting copies of the genes of one's close relatives into future generations.

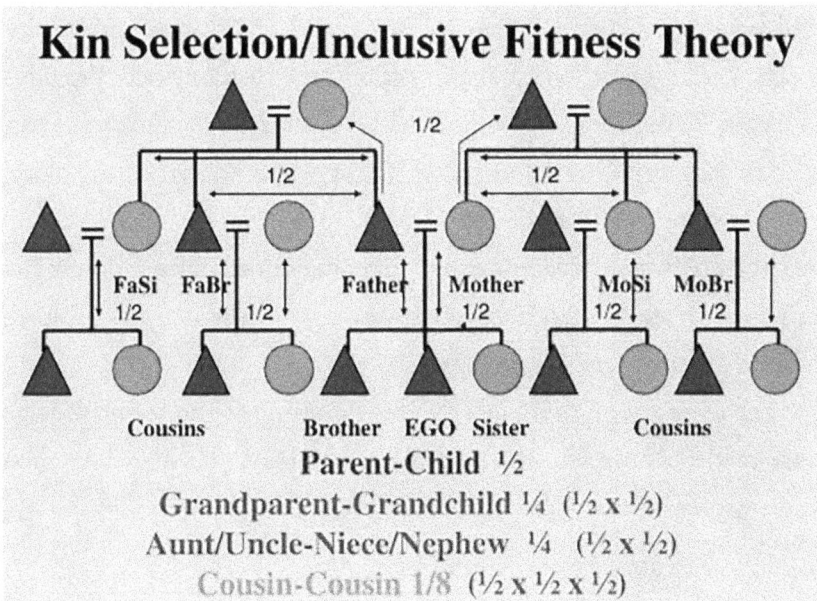

Kin Selection/Inclusive Fitness Theory

Parent-Child ½
Grandparent-Grandchild ¼ (½ x ½)
Aunt/Uncle-Niece/Nephew ¼ (½ x ½)
Cousin-Cousin 1/8 (½ x ½ x ½)

The introduction into scientific thinking of the idea that animal behavior, particularly the behavior of humans, is influenced by genetic evolution has led to intense controversy—and not just in the religious sphere, where, as a rule, people are disinclined to give credence to evolution as the explanation for anything, on account of their tenacious commitment to the idea of a creator.

Outside the sphere of religion (or is it?), the most heated controversy has been in the political sphere, because so many intellectuals, particularly in the social sciences and humanities, are deeply committed to the idea that human nature is a *tabula rasa*, or blank slate, even though these same people generally will accept the idea of genetically influenced behavior in other species.

This commitment goes hand in hand with the belief that human nature is infinitely malleable, and that wise and benevolent leaders will be able to take us all to a higher level of universal prosperity, coupled with environmental protection and social justice, provided everyone is conditioned to believe it and to support the policy agenda.

"Belief morphs into possibility," the saying goes, as if nature places no constraints on what we can *realistically* believe.

The blank slate idea, of course, faces major difficulty if nature has in fact sculpted human behavior in some way, just as it has sculpted human anatomy and physiology.

Let us examine more closely the thinking of the scientists who have made advances in the field of sociobiology, and see where facts and reason take us.

A LITTLE BACKGROUND

There is a remark that was attributed to one Lady Ashley, wife of the Earl of Shaftesbury and a contemporary of Darwin, who, upon being told that Darwin's theory implied that humans and other animals had common ancestors, allegedly responded:

"Let us hope it is not true; but if it is true, let us hope it will not become generally known."

Even though the remark might be apocryphal, it illustrates the unease generally felt at that time around the notion that humans descended from an apelike creature.

The unease has persisted and is still with us. Between the publication of Darwin's *Descent of Man* (1871) and the publication of Wilson's *Sociobiology* (1975), academics first raised the problem of how human social behavior might have evolved, then set it aside as too controversial, and later gradually reintroduced it into the study of biology.

Darwin had argued that sympathy, cooperation, and moral sentiments were products of natural selection, sometimes acting at the level of groups as well as individuals. But among most biologists for many decades, the topic of the effect of evolution on human behavior was considered a third-rail issue—touch it and your career is dead. Speculation on the subject was left largely to social theorists and eugenicists, whose arguments were often ideologically motivated rather than scientific.

We have, for example, the idea of Social Darwinism, often attributed (unfairly) to Herbert Spencer, who did not coin the term. Stated simply, it means that if someone is high in the hierarchy of wealth and power, it's because they are somehow "fitter" and therefore belong there.

Spencer himself was interested in evolution and sought, even before the publication of Darwin's work, to employ evolutionary thinking broadly in his multi-volume magnum opus *System of Synthetic Philosophy*. But others at the time applied his ideas to justify the status quo of power relationships and the use of power to oppress and exploit, in ways that Spencer himself did not approve of.

Interest in the topic of the influence of evolution on behavior started to revive when biologists began reconciling Darwin's ideas about natural selection with Mendelian ideas about genetic inheritance in the 1930s and 1940s.

Researchers such as J.B.S. Haldane demonstrated that Mendelian inheritance could produce the genetic variation Darwin had hypothesized, even though Darwin himself had not come up with any fruitful ideas about the mechanism involved in producing the variation that was necessary to give the selection process something to select.

Theoreticians then began talking about the subject of altruism and the puzzle of why altruistic behavior had evolved in a world of competition for survival and reproduction when resources are scarce. They hit upon the idea that natural selection could, in principle, favor sacrifice for relatives, such as when social insects sacrifice themselves to defend the colony.

Only the brave and foolhardy in those earlier times, however—such as Konrad Lorenz, Karl von Frisch and Niko Tinbergen—went so far as to draw any parallels between human behavior and the behavior of "lower" animals. The trio shared the 1973 Nobel Prize in Medicine for their discoveries about the organization and elicitation of individual and social behavior patterns in animals.

By the 1960s, biologists had turned more seriously to the evolution of cooperation. V.C. Wynne-Edwards, echoing ideas popular at the time and still popular today, proposed that animals, including humans, acted "for the good of the group," but this view was decisively challenged by George C. Williams, who argued that natural selection operates mainly on individuals, and who pointed out that Wynne-Edwards had offered nothing to explain how animals could even *know* what was good for the group, let alone act to promote it.

At the same time, W.D. Hamilton's theory of inclusive fitness offered a powerful explanation of altruism, showing how helping relatives could spread one's genes, which is the thing that natural selection selects for.

Inclusive fitness also probably explains, among other things, why the gene(s) for homosexuality persist, even though desire for a person of the same sex ought to result in fewer offspring. It takes only a small negative differential for any genetic variation to die out. To whatever extent homosexuality is genetically influenced, the negative differential is clearly being offset by something, and inclusive fitness could provide the explanation.

The term *sociobiology* entered the public sphere in a big way when, in 1975, biologist Edward O. Wilson published *Sociobiology: The New Synthesis.*

Professor Wilson's area of study was ants and other social insects. He stated in his introduction that his goal as a scientist was to understand the role of genetics in influencing behavior, and with social insects experimentation is relatively easy to do because insect behavior is rigidly instinctive; so a researcher does not have to be concerned with the added complexity of environmental influence that is present in research about social vertebrates.

Wilson made the observation that the functioning of societies of social vertebrates in many ways resembles the functioning of societies of social insects, even though the individuals in the respective societies are quite different. This suggests that nature has been sculpting social behavior following much the same playbook for all forms of social creatures.

He noted, among other examples, that ant colonies and human cities both contain multiple individuals functioning in a highly integrated way to solve similar problems of communication and resource flow.

He coined the term *eusociality* to describe the tendency to form cooperative, multigenerational groups and argued that this was the decisive step that has allowed both social insects and humans to dominate the planet in biomass and ecological impact.

And humans *are* social vertebrates, as much as we like to think of ourselves as separate and apart from "mere" animals. From the realization that our behavior has roots in natural selection was born the study of what is now known as *evolutionary psychology*, which has given us more powerful explanations of our behavior than what we had before.

It's pretty difficult not to notice that we humans are social vertebrates; it would be remarkable indeed if our society did not share many characteristics of other vertebrate societies. You can try not to notice, of course, by the tried-and-true tactic of arbitrary dichotomizing and the accompanying blatant assertion that "we're different."

Or you can try vilification of those whose conclusions you are reluctant to accept. A notable example of this tactic showed up in the work of biologist Richard Lewontin, a man with a remarkable capacity for doublethink, who was committed to Marxist dogma even though a respected scientist (a *rara avis* indeed), and who dismissed Wilson's work as nothing more than "ideological superstructure" intended to support and justify the societal status quo—an accusation reminiscent of those leveled earlier against Herbert Spencer—and on this basis felt no need to come to grips with, or even acknowledge, the facts and reason employed by Wilson.

It is not uncommon to encounter comparisons from opponents of the science of sociobiology with the now-despised science of eugenics, which of course leads to a comparison with the horrors perpetrated in the name of eugenics by Nazi Germany, where the idea was taken to its logical conclusion.

It's ironic that these accusers have short memories and seem unaware that eugenics was a pet cause, prior to World War II, of the same intellectual tradition of progressivism adhered to by those who are now using these accusations to tar their political opponents.

There is, however, plentiful evidence of the influence of evolution on human behavior. Let's look at a few examples of this phenomenon.

Perception of Beauty

It has long been a firmly held belief in mainstream social science that standards of beauty are wholly arbitrary, just inexplicable fashions that vary over time and between cultures. The evidence is clear, however, that beauty is not just in the eye of the beholder. Men and women with more symmetrical features, for example, are considered more beautiful in every culture. The same is true of such features as clearer skin and thick, glossy hair, and other traits that signal health, vitality, and fertility.

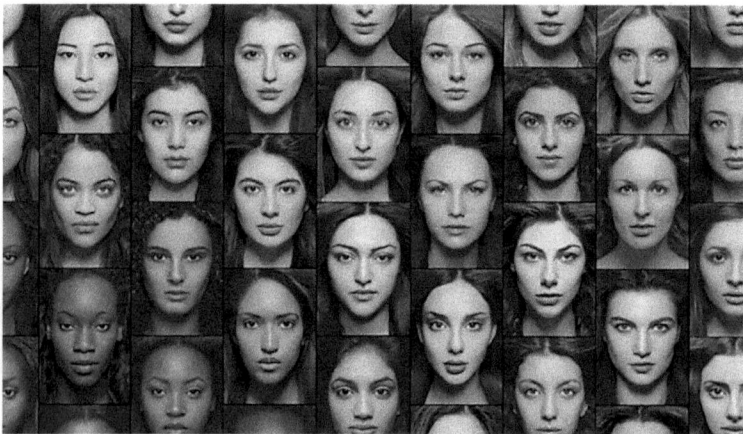

Universally Beautiful

EXPRESSIONS OF EMOTION

The faces of humans in all cultures express emotions in much the same way. You could plunk just about anyone down in an unfamiliar foreign land, and that person would be able to recognize the emotions in the faces of the locals: fear, surprise, anger, joy, disgust, etc. look the same everywhere. We do not have to learn a *new* set of emotional expressions when traveling from one place to another.

Charles Darwin pointed out the deep evolutionary roots of emotional expression in his *The Expression of the Emotions in Man and Animals*, published not long after the publication of *The Origin of Species*.

LANGUAGE ACQUISITION

The eminent linguist Noam Chomsky posited a universal grammar—that is, a common structural basis for language—as a feature of the human animal, with roots in genetic evolution.

The dominant belief before Chomsky published his work was that language acquisition was entirely the product of conditioning of the individual phenotype, and not *genetic* memory,

i.e., the sculpting of the genotype by evolutionary processes. The evidence in support of Chomsky's hypothesis is overwhelming. See, for example, the discussion of this topic in linguist Steven Pinker's book *The Language Instinct.*

The list of commonalities among human cultures that can probably *only* be explained as the result of evolutionary sculpting goes on. As we might expect, much of it is centered on mating: things like the nuclear family; why women tend to be more sexually selective than men; different reasons why men and women find each other sexually appealing; different tendencies in male and female jealousy, with women more concerned about emotional intimacy and men more concerned with physical intimacy; distinct differences between male and female bodily structure and behavioral tendencies; cuteness in children; romantic love, etc.

Resistance to the implications of sociobiology from those in the social sciences and the humanities has frequently taken the form of accusations against biologists saying they are advocating genetic determinism, i.e., that biology equals destiny.

Wilson and other sociobiologists in fact were saying no such thing, and explicitly stated and demonstrated that they were not. You would be hard pressed to find even one example among modern biologists of someone who believes that biology equals destiny.

But in what can only be viewed as a disgraceful episode, social scientists, and even a few biologists, who regarded themselves as gatekeepers of what the public should be allowed to know, subjected Wilson to merciless personal attacks and attempts to discredit the science he presented with their straw man argument.

In the ongoing debate about sociobiology, science will certainly prevail eventually, because delusions do not do well in a scientific environment.

And the science leads to the conclusion that there is indeed some non-erasable writing we cannot ignore on the slate that we have been presuming to be blank.

3

LESSONS FROM FRACTAL GEOMETRY AND NON-LINEAR DYNAMICS

The purpose of the discussion in this chapter is to introduce some elementary features of this fascinating topic, to note the sheer fun of learning about it, and eventually to focus on one particular feature which arises from the study of fractals and non-linear dynamics which is foundational to the notion of societal governance without governors.

Allow me to lead you to the conclusion that I find so interesting, and which I believe to be so applicable to the study of political economy and much else.

Imagine it if you have not seen it, and remember it if you have: a river current flowing into advancing ocean surf. The river's current has kinetic energy and so do the ocean's waves. What happens when these energies tangle?

Find a video, watch it more than once and pay close attention to details. Notice that the energetic tangling of the river's current and the ocean's waves triggers an astonishing amount of complexity, both in the ocean's waves and in the river's current, and things happen that might seem counterintuitive until you see them with your own eyes.

For instance, the ocean's waves continue to propagate up the river against the river's current for quite some distance, unless the current is overwhelmingly powerful. And the river's current flows into and through the advancing waves.

The flowing current and the advancing waves both singly and together sculpt the ocean floor and the riverbed, including the ground on the sides and the bottom of the river's channel, in complex patterns, and the sculpted ground in turn influences the flow of the water, in a dazzlingly complex interplay.

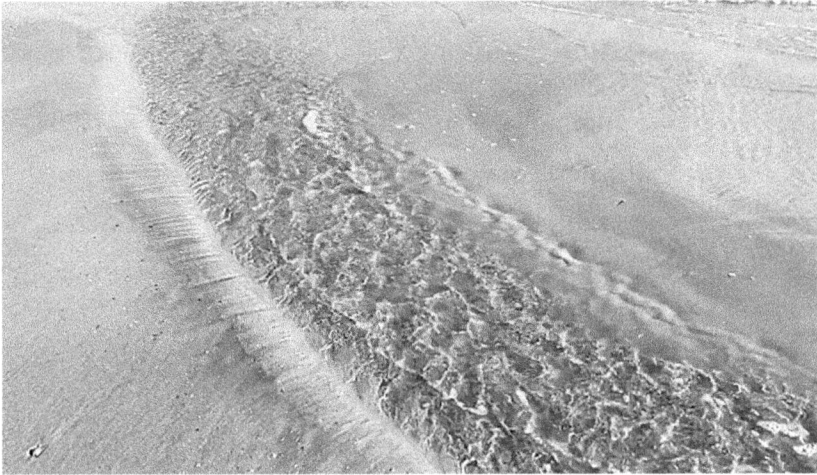

This phenomenon is a lovely example of a dynamical process with fractal characteristics that occurs in nature, one of a vast number of such dynamical processes that occur all around us continually.

For much of earth's recorded history, there have been hints, especially in the world of art, of a level of understanding of what we now call fractals. See for example the waves and the clouds in the famous paintings of Katsushika Hokusai, a Japanese artist who lived a couple of centuries ago, and whose work was introduced to Europeans during his lifetime.

Consider the Asian concepts of yin and yang, which also demonstrate a kind of fractal structure. I am told that any manifestation of yang can be further divided into its own yin and yang (and vice versa), and so on *ad infinitum*. This is an instance of the fractal principle of self-similarity across different scales.

Self-Similarity Across Scale

The spark that in modern times ignited the thinking about non-linear dynamics was struck in the field of weather forecasting. A meteorologist at the Massachusetts Institute of Technology by the name of Edward Norton Lorenz more or less stumbled upon the idea of deterministic chaos, and recognized it as significant.

In a famous story, Lorenz, who was working on computer-assisted numerical weather forecasting, was running some computer simulations of weather outcomes involving a particular set of variables. At one point, he wanted to repeat a simulation that he had already run, but this time he started it in the middle instead of at the beginning, to save time, using as input for the new run the data as it had been printed out at that point in the original run.

To his puzzled amazement, he then observed a significant departure in the results produced by the second run compared to the results of the first run. The explanation for the phenomenon he observed turned out to be that the data taken from halfway through the first run that served as the inputs to start the second run had been rounded. The minute variations between the *actual* numbers from the first run and the *rounded* numbers was enough to send the simulation on a qualitatively different path!

This was an instance of "sensitive dependence on initial conditions", also known as the butterfly effect, and it is a commonly encountered feature in systems where the dynamics are non-linear. Non-linear just means that the magnitude of a response can be out of proportion to the magnitude of the input.

Shortly after Lorenz's heyday, the brilliant and intuitive French mathematician Benoit Mandelbrot published "The Fractal Geometry of Nature". This treatise, with its rigorous quantitative exposition, made a huge impact and opened previously unimagined vistas in science and philosophy.

Mandelbrot knew of Lorenz and his work with deterministic chaos and complex natural patterns; and although he came at the investigation from a different angle, he and Lorenz ended up in pretty much the same place. Both scientists were talking about strange attractors; and Lorenz himself created the Lorenz attractor, which fits the definition of "strange", and another one worth looking up on YouTube. Mandelbrot's geometry of fractals is linked with the dynamics of chaos as introduced by Lorenz.

Both men realized that new mathematical methods of investigating nature were called for. The scope of mathematical descriptions of the natural world had until then been limited to things that can be thought of as "smooth" ("differentiable" in math-speak - think of a sine wave for example, which has a definable tangent at every point along the curve).

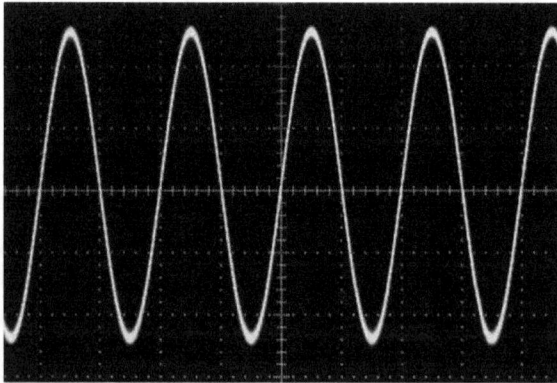

Mandelbrot showed us that we also can employ mathematical methods to describe things that are "rough", i.e., things with corners, which do not have definable tangents at every point along the curve. Have a look at the Weierstrass Function, which is continuous (unbroken), and which has no unique tangent at any point.

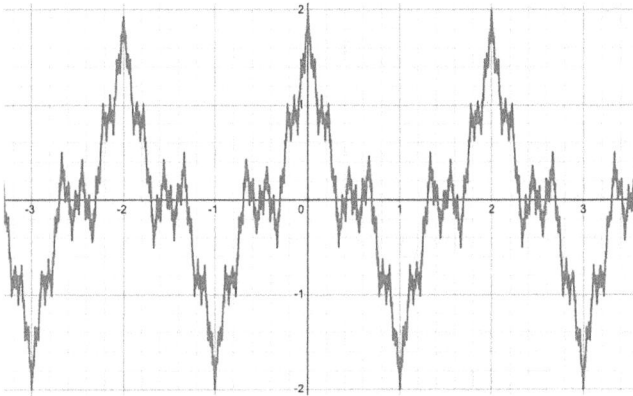

We can also gain insight into turbulent flows.

Think, for example, of the steam rising from your morning cup of coffee. For a certain distance, this steam might rise along a predictable path in what is referred to as a "laminar flow", but it leaves the smooth path and quickly becomes turbulent as it continues to rise. The resulting pattern is so complex and varied that it becomes impossible to predict.

If you can imagine yourself massless and very small, and riding on a particular water molecule within the steam, there is no way that you would be able to predict with any confidence where the molecule you are riding on will be in the near future, if the flow is turbulent, because you would not be able to measure the current state of the molecule with sufficient precision.

Traditional methods of mathematics can deal well with laminar flows, but not so well with turbulent flows.

And although the methods of fractal geometry do not lead us to precise predictions of future developments, they can reveal useful insights into how complex systems evolve, and how the "attractors" and "strange attractors" function within these systems.

I am calling attention to fractal geometry and non-linear dynamics because they reveal something quite valuable as we pursue our aim of creating a meaningful world view, namely that many natural phenomena are not merely difficult to predict, but are *fundamentally* unpredictable; and that any valid world view must take into account this unpredictability.

To understand nature's unpredictability, it's enormously helpful to understand fractals and non-linear dynamics at some level, and especially to understand the nature of the strange attractor.

If you are among the few who can deal with the formal mathematics Mandelbrot gave us, good for you! But even without much training in mathematics, you can still gain useful insights into fractals.

If you wish to go deeper, you might want to begin by reading Mandelbrot's memoir, called *The Fractalist*, which he worked on all his life, and which was published shortly after he died in 2010.

His memoir reveals fascinating details about his intellectual journey from childhood on, his formal education, his work as a mathematician, and about his rare intellectual gifts, particularly his unusual ability to create visualizations of mathematical concepts as a key to deep understanding.

So let's step onto the road of understanding the phenomenon of the strange attractor, and why it is significant. Here are a few basic concepts in fractal geometry.

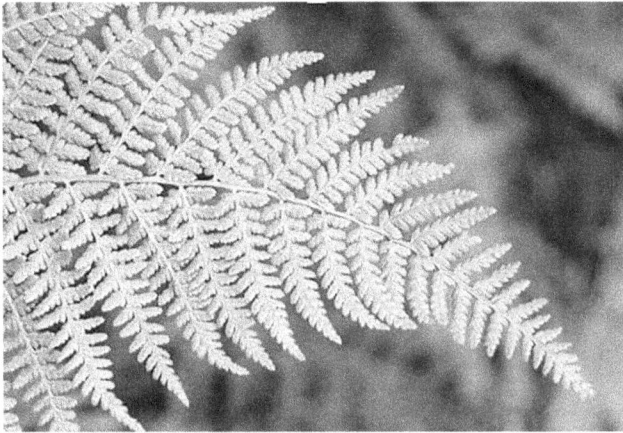

The Fractal Geometry of Nature

One key concept, already alluded to above, is *self-similarity across scales*. An example that helps to illustrate this idea is the structure of a fern, which is a leaf that is made up of smaller copies of itself.

For a truly dramatic illustration of self-similarity across scales, search YouTube for "Mandelbrot Set Zoom", and notice the similarity of the patterns being generated as you zoom in or out.

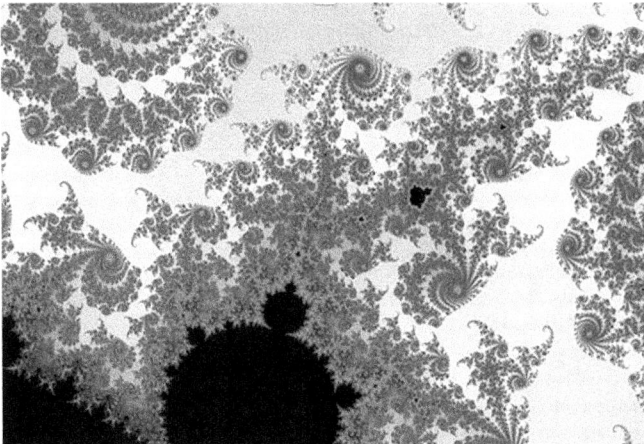

The Mandelbrot set is probably his most widely known contribution, and it is generated by a large number of iterations of a relatively simple equation (at least if you consider a discussion involving complex numbers to be simple), where the outputs of one iteration are used as inputs for the next iteration. The images look the same somehow, i.e. they have the same general shapes, no matter how far you zoom in or out, and old patterns such as the original beetle, called a "baby Mandelbrot", reoccur in a way that is almost but not quite identical to the original.

Another useful concept as we build an understanding of fractals is *fractal dimension*. You might have encountered a fractal image somewhere or other, and noticed that its fractal dimension might be given as, for example, 1.7, or 2.4. What does such a thing mean?

We all know there are three spatial dimensions in the world we live and move in, and apparently one temporal one. Common sense tells us that any object exists in some *integer* number of dimensions. Are mathematicians just wacko?

I hope you will be happy to hear that there is a useful meaning of fractal dimension that is not all that difficult to understand, which does not contradict the intuition we have of spatial dimensions, and which will help you to understand the rest of the discussion about fractal dimension.

Here's a simple, easy-to-follow example:

Think of an ideal two-dimensional plane, like a sheet of paper with zero thickness, and to begin with think of it as an empty space.

Then imagine that you place a simple object in that idealized space. Let's use an equilateral triangle. An equilateral triangle can be transformed step by step into a fractal object known as a Koch snowflake, introduced to the world by Swedish mathematician Nils Fabian Helge von Koch, an early contributor to the study of fractals.

The first step of the triangle's transformation is accomplished by replacing the middle third of each of the three sides with a new outward-pointing equilateral triangle. The first iteration of this transformation will give you a six-pointed star.

Transform the figure again by applying the same algorithm we just used in Step 1 to each straight-line segment all around the new figure. Do this again and again as many times as you like, applying the recipe to the increasing number of shorter and shorter straight-line segments.

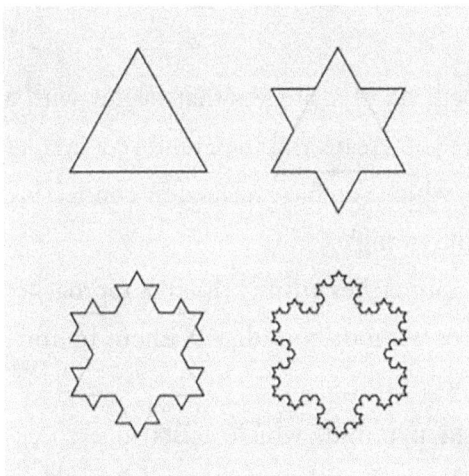

Note that each iteration uses up a little more of the two-dimensional space in which the object exists. But it *never* takes up *all* of the available area even as the number of iterations becomes very large, and the limit of the proportion of the two-dimensional space it does take up as the number of iterations approaches infinity is its fractal dimension.

In the case of the Koch snowflake, the fractal dimension turns out to be about 1.262, and the area of the snowflake converges on 8/5 of the area of the original triangle.

If you find this stuff interesting, I encourage you to also have a look at the Sierpinski triangle, which exists in a two-dimensional space and has a fractal dimension of 1.585.

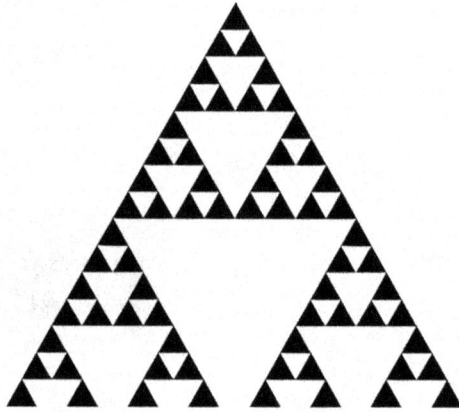

This object is created by a repetition of a process that begins with a filled equilateral triangle, where you create and then remove a smaller triangle from the filled portion, which you have formed by connecting the midpoints of each side of the triangle.

As the number of iterations approaches infinity the area approaches zero, but the perimeter increases without bound. "Without bound" means that there is no finite upper limit.

Then look at the Sierpinski pyramid, which exists in a three-dimensional space, but which has a fractal dimension of 2.0. How weird is that?

The pyramid is formed in a way similar to the triangle, except you are successively removing tetrahedra from a three-dimensional space instead of triangles from a two-dimensional space. The volume approaches zero as the number of iterations approaches infinity, and the area increases without bound.

Now we get to the *really* good stuff.

Let's elaborate on the term "strange attractor", mentioned above. This is the concept that has arisen from the study of fractal geometry and from the study of non-linear dynamics that *most* helps us to get it why natural phenomena can be so unpredictable.

A simple attractor is any set of points around which the results of a dynamical process may gather. Examples would include planetary motion and pendulum motion.

An example of a dynamical process that results in a *strange* attractor would be the relative proportions of the populations of predators and prey. Think for example of coyotes and rabbits.

If there are a lot of rabbits, coyotes will kill and eat a lot of them, leading to an increase in the number of coyotes. But since there now aren't as many rabbits left, they will become more difficult for the coyotes to find, and this puts the brakes on the number of coyotes who can survive and reproduce.

Fewer coyotes then results in more rabbits, and so on in a repetitive dynamical process, in which neither population is likely to either explode or go extinct. The proportions of rabbits and coyotes will settle in around a set of figures, and this set of figures is a strange attractor.

It's a *strange* attractor because trajectories of populations never repeat exactly, even though they are confined to a particular region in phase space, and the system exhibits fractal characteristics. If you plot the trajectories on a graph, it will typically resemble the butterfly shape similar to the shape revealed in the Lorenz attractor.

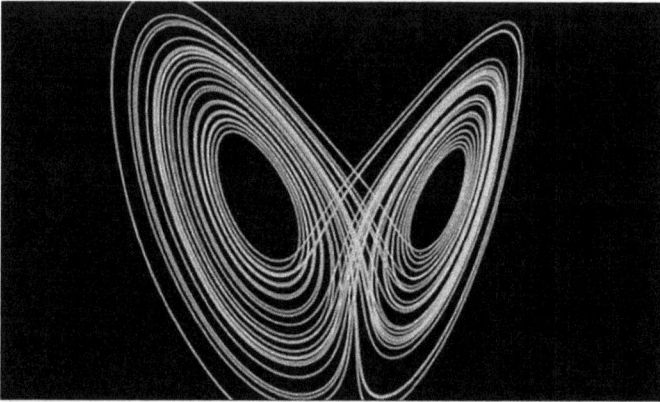

This strange attractor embodies the balance in each population between growth and decline. The populations rise and fall *unpredictably*, even though it's a *deterministic* system.

And now we are getting close to the heart of the matter, and we can explain why so many of the phenomena in the natural world (including the world of human society, which is as natural as anything else) are unpredictable, even when deterministic.

A dynamical process centering upon a strange attractor has the feature of "sensitive dependence on initial conditions", sometimes referred to as the "butterfly effect". Very small changes in initial conditions can lead to very large changes in future conditions (and *vice versa*) and to qualitatively different developmental paths.

What are the implications of the butterfly effect on the effectiveness of weather forecasting, or economic forecasting?

Let us say for example that you would like to make a forecast of some future state of the economy based on measurements of the values of the variables in the current state of the economy, such as output, employment, investment, inflation, etc.

Your reason for making the forecast would be to enable an effective intervention in economic activity in such a way that good outcomes will result.

If you have been paying attention in the real world, you know of course that economic forecasting is notoriously unreliable. The jokes abound: one famous quip was that the only thing economic forecasters have so far accomplished was to make weather forecasting (or fortune-telling) look respectable. Another quip was that economic forecasters have been able to predict nine out the last five recessions.

The principle of sensitive dependence on initial conditions, the butterfly effect, gives us insight into why it has been, is now, and always will be true that economic forecasting is intractable, and would still be intractable even if we were to get better and better at modeling the relationships among the variables.

The problem that *must* be solved if we want a reliable forecast, and which *cannot* in practice be solved, is that the current value of each economic variable must be measured with *infinite* precision (which would take an infinite amount of time) in order for a forecast to produce results you can trust. It ought to be obvious that we will never be able do anything like that in practice, and merely getting the measurements close doesn't help.

Creating a reliable forecast would be a necessary first step in the attempt to control economic outcomes. If it's not possible to produce a reliable forecast, it ought to be *abundantly* clear that we cannot hope, ever, to control outcomes.

And even if we did have the ability to produce a reliable forecast, further problems and failures would arise when we attempted to carry out the intervention, and for the same reason that forecasts fail, namely the butterfly effect.

We need to *stop* going back to the drawing board. We must find an entirely new approach to governance if we seriously desire a better world for ourselves and our progeny.

How about governance without governors?

4

VALUE AND PRICE

If we wish to make progress toward a new paradigm of governance, another fundamental concept we must understand is value: what it is and how it comes into existence.

Value is a key concept for us to understand because, in the broadest sense, it is value that keeps us going, helps us to create progeny, and gives us opportunities to make our lives better; and more value is better than less value, which provides us with a reliable guide to decision-making as long as we understand what value is and what it is not.

As recently as a few hundred years ago, economists were positing two different types of value and having a lot of difficulty reconciling them: (1) value in use and (2) value in exchange.

How could water, for example, have an exchange value at or near zero, while diamonds exchange for great sums of money, even though water, being essential for life, has greater use value?

Economist Adam Smith called this the "paradox of value," and he and other early economists did not succeed in producing a satisfactory explanation for the phenomenon.

Economist Karl Marx concluded that the paradox of value was merely an example of the contradictions that inevitably arise in a capitalist system and made no attempt to resolve it; apparently, establishing grounds for condemnation of what he called capitalism was the important point as far as he was concerned.

Later economists, however, *did* resolve the problem as part of the marginal revolution in the study of economics, which began in the late 19th century and introduced the concept of utility. The resolution rested on the realization that value in exchange depends on marginal utility, and that value in use rests on total utility. There is no paradox.

The reason that water generally has so little exchange value is its abundance—at the margin, one additional unit of water adds very little to someone's total utility. And the reason that diamonds have so much more exchange value than water is that diamonds are not as abundant as water—at the margin, one additional diamond adds a lot to someone's total utility. So prices (exchange values) reflect marginal utility and not total utility.

But let's not get ahead of ourselves.

Early attempts to get a grip on the concept of value centered around labor. Under a labor theory of value, the proposition is that the value of something is equal to the value of the labor that went into its production; or, as Adam Smith framed it, the value of something is equal to the value of the labor that someone must perform in order to earn enough to buy it.

Although there is some plausibility to the musings about labor being the source of value, not everything that *needs* to fit into the conceptual framework of a labor theory of value *actually* fits.

Most notably, we are obliged to explain how the value of the man-made inputs to the production process—sometimes referred to as the "means of production" or "real capital"—fits into this conceptual framework.

Clearly, a laborer coupled with inputs such as machines can produce far more than a laborer working without those inputs; a farmer with a tractor can till more acreage than a farmer with a sharp stick.

We can try to rescue the labor theory by proposing that the value of capital inputs just reflects the labor that was used to produce *those* inputs. This claim, though, seems a bit preposterous on its face, on account of the magnitude of the additional output the capital input enables compared to the relatively small value of the labor it took to produce the capital good.

Marx's labor theory of value, and with it pretty much all of Marxist theory, was dealt a fatal blow during the marginal revolution, when Austrian economist Eugen von Boehm-Bawerk pointed out an unresolvable contradiction in Marx's work involving what became known as the "transformation problem".

And American economist Paul Samuelson, a towering figure in the profession in the mid-20th century, demonstrated mathematically that Marx's theory was internally contradictory.

Samuelson called Marx's attempt to resolve the transformation problem an "algebraic illusion." Later on he even remarked that Marx's theory was a "swan song" of an outdated paradigm, because marginalist economics could generate consistent value/price relationships while Marx's labor theory could not.

As we all know now, of course, the labor theory of value, though dead, has not remained in its grave; it has become an *undead* idea and still wanders the land, eating people's brains.

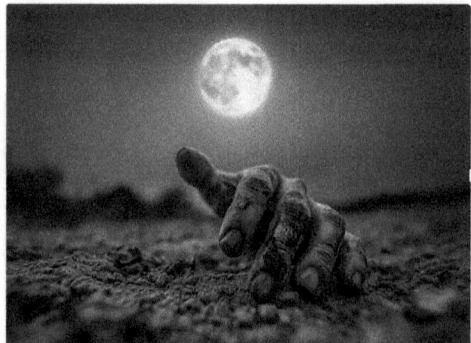

To a disciple of Marx, the labor theory of value simply *must* be true in order to support the desired conclusion, which is that the workers are producing all of the *surplus* value, and that the owners of capital are taking what rightly belongs to the workers when they receive profits over and above the value of the labor embodied in the capital.

And this failure by the followers of Marx to acknowledge clear facts and sound reasoning defines the point where Marxism began to segue from serious political and economic inquiry into the quasi-religious doctrine we observe today, which I have begun calling Marxianity.

Adherents to the labor theory of value have clung to the *conclusion* of their argument in spite of the fact that the argument itself has been shown to be fatally flawed. And the backpedaling and revisionism displayed by these disciples, and their ability to discover class struggle wherever they look, have been quite impressive.

We can gain insight into the way Marxianity has evolved, and into its ongoing appeal, from the writings of American author Michael Shermer, who argued in his book "The Believing Brain", that the same mental processes underlie such things as religious beliefs, belief in conspiracy theories, grand social theories and political ideologies.

Shermer pointed out that the human brain is pattern-seeking. We're hard-wired to find order, structure, and causality, and we "find" these things even in data and anecdotes that are actually random. And we then tend to imagine that intentional actors lie behind the imagined patterns.

These evolved tendencies might have improved our odds of survival in earlier times, but they can misfire in modern settings and lead to all sorts of mischief.

Marxian ideologues who retain the labor theory of value do so not because it is compelling, but because it supports a normative critique of capitalism which they treat as dogma (and it's not entirely clear what the "capitalism" label refers to). Abandoning the labor theory of value would fatally undermine the basis of the assertions about exploitation, surplus value, the wage-profit frontier, and class conflict.

And as with religion or conspiracy theory, the appeal lies not so much in the validity of the explanation as in the emotional certainty it provides, and in the sense of membership in a community where everyone sees things as they "really are."

Marxianity continues to inspire, in spite of having no intellectual foundation, precisely because of how our brains have evolved to form beliefs.

In spite of its obsolescence in the world of science, the labor theory of value is still quite influential in areas of endeavor where doing good science is not the point. There can be little doubt that this concept will eventually go the way of the geocentric model of the universe, but it presently retains its grip, probably because it can serve as the foundation for many simple, easy-to-understand, wrong answers to complex questions in political economy.

But let's move on and say more about the subjective theory of value that emerged from the marginalist revolution.

The subjective theory of value says that things don't have an objective, intrinsic worth. Instead, the value of things is continuously socially constructed. The value of a thing depends on how strongly people *want* the thing, and how strongly they want it compared to how much they want substitutes.

In a modern economy, we don't each trade directly with others based on our personal wants, as we might have done in older times under a barter system. Instead, we now mostly use a price system of resource allocation.

It has been quipped that if the ancient Greeks had understood the price system, they would have deified it, such is its power as a spontaneous coordination mechanism.

Prices act like a set of signals—signals that are useful, even vital, to both buyers and sellers.

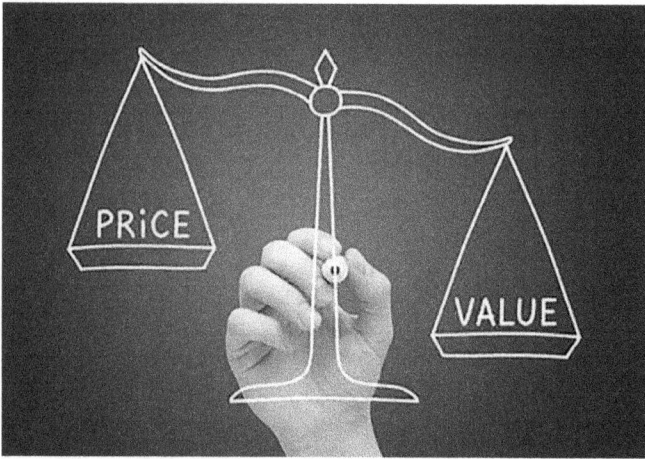

When something is in short supply, or if lots of people want that something, some of them will be willing to pay more to get it, which pushes its price up. This price increase acts as an automatic dampener on quantity demanded, as fewer and fewer of those at the margin are willing to pay an increasingly higher price. The higher price also acts as a signal to suppliers to produce more.

When fewer people want it, or when it's very plentiful, the price falls, and the lower price acts as a signal to suppliers to produce less and a signal to consumers to buy more.

Theorists tell us—and it has been repeatedly demonstrated—that a price system operates in a way that discovers distributed information more quickly and completely than can be matched by any other method of gathering information that we know of.

Witness, for example, the success of prediction markets in outperforming pollsters when it comes to calling elections.

Behavioral economists such as Nobel laureate Vernon L. Smith have demonstrated how a pricing system routinely discovers distributed information about values and prices in an experimental setting that mimics real-world activity.

A market translates millions of individual subjective judgments of value into one clear signal, which we call the market price—a consensus estimate of value.

Knowledge of the price of a resource guides decisions about how much of the resource should go where. If apartment rent rises, for example, it's a sign that more people want apartments or that there is a shortage of apartments at the lower rent. Renters notice this signal and adjust: they might stop looking, they might look for substitutes, or they might just pay the higher rent. At the same time, builders are incentivized to bring more apartments to market.

So the price system works as a kind of automatic coordination mechanism. Nobody has to know of or agree on exactly why people want what they want; each person just acts on their own preferences. A market price reflects all of that scattered, subjective information and guides resources toward their most highly valued uses.

The same reasoning applies to wages, which is what we call the price of labor.

Just like with goods, the value of someone's work isn't fixed in the job itself. Instead, it ultimately depends on how much people (in this case, employers, customers, or society at large) subjectively value what that work produces.

If, for example, lots of people want fancy coffee drinks and are willing to pay high prices for them, then coffee shops can afford to hire more baristas. But since making lattes is a skill many people can learn quickly, the wage for that work tends to remain modest.

If there's a sudden boom in demand for computer chips, the work of skilled chip designers becomes very valuable to companies. And because chip design is not a skill many people can learn quickly, and because firms are competing to hire them, wages for chip engineers rise.

The price system coordinates all of this automatically. Wages function as a translation of subjective value into the incentives that face both workers and employers.

By looking at the wages that are offered, workers learn where their time and skills are most valued.

By looking at their success in attracting workers, employers learn the amount of wages they must offer to attract the workers they wish to hire.

And thus society's limited pool of human effort gets directed toward the tasks that all of us together value most highly, even though no central authority has to—or can—decide who should work where.

It is responses to *natural* incentives that direct the energy flows in a market economy. The energy flows organize the sociome and cause the system to function in such a way that value is produced efficiently—i.e., getting the most bang for the buck—and to work automatically, as long as most of us, most of the time, respect property rights and the sanctity of contract, and as long as we have a legal system that enforces these things in the relatively rare circumstances where people do not respect them.

Governance, mostly without a governor.

And perhaps just as importantly, in a market economy we are all free to follow the hard-wired, evolved impulses of generosity and benevolence most of us feel toward those among us who find themselves in unfortunate circumstances through no fault of their own and who deserve our help. And without any governors to preempt our decisions (and take a cut for themselves), we can send our help in the direction we choose.

We should note that the issue of caring for the less fortunate has been a sticking point for the increasing numbers of people who have at least begun acknowledging the ability of a market economy to create wealth like no other system we know, but who are concerned that a market economy might be a heartless system in practice, and that those in need would be neglected and abandoned. Many of us seem to have trouble believing that the needy would be adequately cared for unless the care is the responsibility of the institution of government.

But the fact is that before the relatively recent development of state-sponsored welfare, the needy were cared for by various private arrangements. And even if some people slipped through the cracks and did not receive care, we have to acknowledge that some people *still* slip through the cracks. And evidence suggests that the current systems are more vulnerable to cheaters and free riders than the older systems.

We do not want to compare actual private welfare with a perfect alternative; we want to compare it with an actual alternative if we want the comparison to be meaningful. Let's not sacrifice an actual good because of an imaginary perfect.

And given the enormously greater value that is generated in a modern market economy than in earlier times, private welfare arrangements are likely to be even *more* effective than earlier private welfare arrangements.

We should not let overblown doubts about the care of the less fortunate stand in the way of achieving governance without governors. We can all be better off.

5

PROPERTY

If we wish to understand the functioning of our sociome, another fundamental concept that we must understand on a deep level is property.

The right to property is one of the three essential components of human rights proposed by the English philosopher John Locke, along with the right to liberty and the right to life. But what exactly is "property"?

In *any* type of society, not just ours, there has to be *some* method of deciding what portion everyone gets from what everyone produces, and there are, in the broadest sense, two alternatives: 1) authority based on hierarchy, or 2) ownership based on individual liberty.

The reason there has to be a method for deciding who gets what is contained in the word *scarcity*. We need to understand what scarcity is and what it is not if we wish to achieve clarity of understanding.

First of all, we must distinguish *scarcity* from *shortage*. And although these terms are often used interchangeably, calling two different things by the same name leads to confusion in an area where clarity is essential.

Of course, if your aim is to *sow* confusion, conflating these words is a way to do so—with proven effectiveness.

A *shortage* is defined as a condition in a market where the quantity demanded is greater than the quantity supplied at a particular price. A shortage is typically temporary, because shortages (and their opposite, surpluses) can be eliminated by changes in prices or by changes in supply and demand conditions. A shortage is therefore a temporary market condition and not a fundamental condition of life.

Scarcity, on the other hand, is defined as the difference between the total amount of stuff that there is to go around, and the total amount of stuff we collectively want; and there is strong reason to assume that scarcity will always be with us as a fundamental condition of life, simply because the list of things we collectively want is endless and because resources are limited.

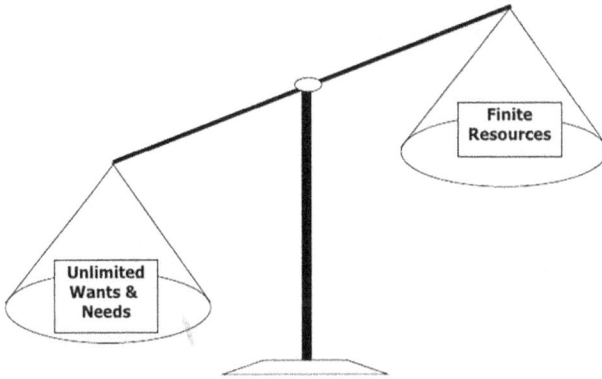

In a hypothetical world like Alice's Restaurant, where scarcity is not a thing, there would be no need for a method to decide who gets what, because we would all be able to get anything we want (except Alice).

In our world today the concept of property is a muddy one with many connotations, many of them evil, so we need to work through the idea and understand exactly what property means for our purposes, and how it creates functionality within the sociome. We must separate the baby from the bathwater.

Let's begin by reviewing what some notables have said about property.

Nathaniel Hawthorne wrote, "What we call real estate - the solid ground to build a house on - is the broad foundation on which nearly all the guilt of this world rests. A man will commit almost any wrong - he will heap up an immense pile of wickedness, as hard as granite, and which will weigh as heavily upon his soul, to eternal ages - only to build a great, gloomy, dark-chambered

mansion, for himself to die in, and for his posterity to be miserable in".

Bathwater.

Robert Ingersoll wrote, "Don't you know that if people could bottle the air, they would? Don't you know that they would allow thousands and millions to die for want of breath, if they could not pay for air?

Bathwater.

George Bernard Shaw wrote, "Property is organized robbery".

Bathwater.

Bertrand Russell wrote, "... it is preoccupation with possessions, more than anything else, that prevents men from living freely and nobly.... Possession means taking or keeping some good thing which another is prevented from enjoying...".

Mostly bathwater.

On the other hand, many people believe that observance of property rights is one of humankind's most civilizing practices. In a world of scarcity such as ours, if property rights are well-defined, widely observed and honored, there would be fewer disputes over who gets what than in a world without property rights.

Nobel economics laureate Elinor Ostrom wrote, "When we see property simply as exclusion, we miss its moral and cooperative dimensions. Property can be a system of shared stewardship."

She declared further, "No single center of authority can adequately govern the many commons of the world. Property rights are human creations that evolve with the problems they are meant to solve."

Baby. So much wisdom in those statements!

And let us note that Russell made a glaring omission in his characterization of possession, an omission which is not surprising coming from a member of the British ruling class who himself has never engaged in production and commerce, and one which we *must* look at in all of its implications if we want to have a chance of developing deep understanding.

He said that property means "taking" or "keeping" a good thing; what he *failed* to mention is that property can also mean, and more often than not does mean, "producing" a good thing.

Objections to taking can be valid; but it is quite a different matter when keeping means each of us keeping the value we ourselves have created in the course of fair competition.

If we believe in the right to life and the right to liberty, we ought also to believe in the right to property, because without such a right the promises of the rights to life and liberty ring hollow. If someone has the authority to take our property, they have the power thereby to effectively take our liberty and ultimately our life.

As John Adams wrote, "Property must be secured, or liberty cannot exist."

Let us then examine the concept of property more broadly and deeply, and see if we can make sense of the concept in a way we can all find helpful.

In a social order defined by hierarchy (think of a system of feudalism, or life on a plantation), authority, based on rank, preempts the choices of lower-ranked persons. The lord and master, and those to whom he has delegated authority, dictate who gets what for people of lesser rank. In a hierarchical society, you have takers and victims.

In a social order defined by property, contractual arrangements among people who are equal by custom and/or under the law determine who gets what, under a system of pricing. In a property-based society, there are traders rather than takers and victims.

The quotations above represent the thoughts of some of those who have speculated that perhaps we could have a functioning society without either property or hierarchy. They claim to believe that in an ideal world people could exist by simply sharing what they produce. Think of John Lennon's wistful "Imagine."

This sounds nice, but it fails to address the problem of scarcity. In a society without either ownership or authority, how would scarce resources be rationed?

You cannot just assume the problem away and make lofty, pious pronouncements about how everyone has a right to as much stuff as they need, when they need it. If you were to add up everyone's "needs," it would inevitably exceed how much stuff there is.

Some have proposed that, to make attainment of the ideal of common ownership more practicable, the state might own the means of production on behalf of the people and engage in top-down economic planning.

Experiments along these lines in the recent past, however, have produced only poverty, tyranny, misery, and early death for the people unfortunate enough to have been the subjects of the experiments.

The reasons for the failures of these experiments are now well understood, even if not universally accepted by the few remaining diehards, and lead to the conclusion that a system of state control of production coupled with economic planning can *never* work.

What we now well understand is, first of all, that an economic planner cannot gather the necessary information as quickly and completely as a pricing system based on supply and demand, and secondly, that in a planned economy the necessary incentives for individual behavior are absent, and are often even perverse. And in the absence of effective natural incentives, the go-to incentive becomes coercion.

And in a more general sense, what we now have reason to believe, due both to historical experience and to the study of natural systems, is that the sheer amount of complexity a planner would have to deal with is many orders of magnitude greater than we used to believe, and far greater than we can ever hope to deal with using authoritarian methods.

It seems to me that proponents of common ownership are guilty of the commonly encountered means-and-ends fallacy, i.e., the idea that we can choose the ends and, with sufficient authority, force the ends into existence, whereas in truth we can only choose means directly, after which processes of evolution will determine the ends.

And as for the idea that sharing is a viable substitute for hierarchy or property, it is also pretty certain that the "thinkers" of these ideas have not spent much time around young children. If you have spent time around children who have been taught that sharing is a major virtue, you have to have noticed that children are far more likely to apply the principle of sharing to *other* kids' stuff than to their *own* stuff. If they see something they want, they just invoke the not-to-be-questioned principle that the other child is supposed to share.

Until the advocates of common ownership inhabiting our ivory towers come up with a workable method for coming to grips with scarcity, their arguments cannot be considered to have merit.

Denotatively, the concept of property has a simple and straightforward meaning. Connotatively, there are multiple meanings—the word "property" conjures up different visions for different people.

The simple and straightforward meaning is that property represents an agreement among people in a community to recognize and respect the exclusive right of another community member to use and dispose of some tangible or intangible asset. That is the definition of ownership.

Things are seldom quite as simple in practice as described above, of course, because some uses of assets might create incidental effects, also known as externalities, which we then need to make part of the equation.

In other words, actions an owner might take for the purpose of creating private benefits can create social costs—think, for example, of adding a second story to your house, which is great for you but might block your neighbor's view.

It's likewise true that actions aimed at creating private benefits can create social benefits—think, for example, of planting flowers and shrubs around your house, which is great for you and which your neighbors will also enjoy for free.

The brilliant UCLA economist Harold Demsetz made a valuable, seminal contribution to thinking about the evolution of property rights. In a 1967 paper, *Toward a Theory of Property Rights*, he showed how private ownership can evolve from communal ownership as a way of dealing with externalities that arise from the communal use of a resource, such as land that is being used for hunting and gathering.

In an analysis of a case study of Indian tribes in Labrador by anthropologist Eleanor Burke Leacock, he shows how and why ownership by individuals and families came into being in relation to hunting and trapping rights. His paper is a must-read for anyone seriously interested in the topic.

The thesis of this paper is as follows:

Just about any action by any individual in any type of society is going to have some effect, either harmful or beneficial, on a person or persons besides the individual taking the action.

In a society based on the communal use of a resource, these harmful or beneficial effects will be just someone's tough luck or good luck, respectively, until the cost of doing nothing becomes greater than the cost of doing something to influence the person taking the action to take a different action.

Bringing to bear a consideration of external effects on the decisions of the actor is called internalization. Internalization ideally takes the form of the emergence of a customary or legally enforced property right. As Demsetz states this crucial insight in his paper, "Property rights develop when the gains from internalization become larger than the cost of internalization."

For example, think of a rural agricultural area where the population is sparse. In such circumstances people would gather and burn whatever fuel was close at hand—wood, dried manure, peat, etc.—for purposes of cooking and heating. Burning the fuel, in addition to providing energy for the home, uses resources that then become unavailable to others, and it produces smoke.

Nobody has much of an incentive to do anything about these external effects as long as population remains sparse, because neighboring families are still able to find ample fuel for themselves, and the distant smoke of a few neighbors is not particularly bothersome.

But as population becomes denser, the external effects of fuel usage begin to make more of a difference to the neighbors. Eventually it becomes worth it to develop a custom or enact a statute that will internalize the costs, i.e., to cause each user of fuel to take into account the effects of their use on others, e.g., by limiting or pricing the gathering rights and/or by making the emission of smoke costly to the emitter.

What about the argument, put forward by many of the thinkers quoted above, and first stated by Pierre-Joseph Proudhon, that "Property is theft"? I believe there actually is a defensible rationale behind this slogan, even though in the case of Proudhon and his contemporaries it was nominally based on the now-discredited labor theory of value.

It is certainly possible to gain property by an act of theft, and history is not lacking in examples; but the idea that all property has been gained by acts of theft, or the idea that obtaining exclusive rights to use property itself constitutes theft because of the "exclusive" part—we're getting a little silly. These are ideas that make sense only within ivory towers.

So until someone figures out a way to make common ownership coupled with sharing work in practice, the choice is stark: would you rather live in a society where the problem of scarcity is dealt with by queueing or forced rationing? Or would you rather live in a society where the problem of scarcity is dealt with by contractual arrangements under a system of pricing based on property rights?

We cannot ignore the problem of scarcity, and if we try, reality will make itself felt. Reality does not just guide with an invisible hand; it also trips with an invisible foot.

6

LEARNING FROM
GAME THEORY

Consider a typical agitprop post on social media: "Billionaires are hoarding the wealth while millions of people go hungry".

I used to tell my students that if I could wave a magic wand and change just one thing in the world, my wish would be to make zero-sum thinking vanish.

If this agitprop post seems to makes sense to you (even in a world where fewer and fewer people are actually going hungry), you are envisioning a finite pie that is being cut up and passed around.

What we too often fail to envision is that we can make bigger pies, and we can make more of them. And if that's the case, then anyone can get more by simply producing more, and no one is worse off. And as long as those among us who are getting a lot more are doing it fair and square, i.e., without employing force, fraud, or subsidies, then we should regard it as a non-issue.

And that's not all. The way we conceive of "more" is not limited to mere physical quantities but can also extend to the amount of utility derived from consumption.

The brilliant Irish economist Francis Edgeworth explained how a different distribution of existing quantities, based on voluntary exchange, can create greater total utility—more utility for me and more utility for you.

The key to understanding his argument is the concept of diminishing marginal utility, i.e., the idea that as you consume more and more of a good or service, the additional utility provided at the margin is less than the utility derived from previous consumption. Thus we can find someone to trade with for mutual gain if they have more than enough of something we still want and we have more than enough of something they still want, to oversimplify slightly.

Edgeworth created a graphical representation of this type of trade for mutual gain with his famous Edgeworth Box. The Edgeworth Box illustrates how two rational agents can achieve mutually beneficial outcomes through voluntary exchange, and that's an important thing to understand. However, it is a *static* model that assumes cooperation and trust already exist.

Robert Axelrod's theory of games, by contrast, explores how such cooperation

and trust can emerge and endure among self-interested actors through repeated interactions.

In his studies of the Iterated Prisoner's Dilemma game, Axelrod showed that strategies based on reciprocity—such as the "Tit for Tat" strategy—can initiate and then sustain cooperation over time by rewarding trust and punishing defection. Thus, while the Edgeworth Box depicts the ideal results of successful cooperation, Axelrod's framework explains the behavioral mechanisms that make such outcomes achievable in practice. Together, they reveal that the efficient exchange envisioned by economic theory depends on the evolution of trust and stable cooperation as described by game theory.

Axelrod's work deserves a lot of attention because it deals with a topic so many of us have trouble with—namely, the topic of competition.

Many of us believe that competition and cooperation are opposites, and that competition is bad and cooperation is good. Competition is regarded as part of our animal past that is best left behind as something incompatible with human morality—nature red in tooth and claw, in the words of Lord Tennyson.

But this is a shallow concept of competition, and if we give it a little extra thought, it becomes evident that competition has gotten a bad rap and that there is more to competition than just predation and warfare. Axelrod's work is notable because it demonstrates how cooperation can emerge among self-interested individuals, as it is possible to win without defeating anyone - symbiosis.

Let's take a closer look at how Axelrod showed this to be true, using the Iterated Prisoner's Dilemma (IPD) as a model of repeated strategic interaction.

In 1980, Axelrod invited leading game theorists, economists, political scientists, and mathematicians to submit computer programs that would play repeated rounds of the prisoner's dilemma against each other. The results were published first in a 1981 paper and then in his book *The Evolution of Cooperation*, first published in 1984.

Each program had to decide during each round whether to cooperate (C) or defect (D), knowing that payoffs depended on the choices made by both programs.

Between any two players, there were four possibilities: CC, CD, DC, and DD, with a payoff matrix that gave the most points for a defection if your opponent cooperated, and the fewest points to you if you were thus suckered. If you both defected, you would be slightly better off than had only your opponent defected. If you both cooperated, you wouldn't get as many points as you would if you could sucker your opponent, but the sum of the points available to you both would be maximized.

Payoff Matrix (Axelrod's Prisoner's Dilemma)

	Player B Cooperates	Player B Defects
Player A Cooperates	A: R = 3 B: R = 3	A: S = 0 B: T = 5
Player A Defects	A: T = 5 B: S = 0	A: P = 1 B: P = 1

Meaning of the symbols

- T (Temptation to defect) = 5
- R (Reward for mutual cooperation) = 3
- P (Punishment for mutual defection) = 1
- S (Sucker's payoff) = 0

Every program that was submitted played every other program many times, with scores averaged over the tournament.

The surprising winner was a simple strategy called Tit for Tat, submitted by Russian-American mathematician Anatol Rapoport, a leading researcher in systems theory and conflict resolution in the twentieth century.

Most of the programs that had been submitted attempted strategic defections in order to capture the large gains available if your opponent cooperated and you defected.

Rapoport's program cooperated on the first move and then copied the opponent's previous move thereafter.

His program was nice (it never defected first and it never tried to sucker anyone), it was retaliatory (it punished defection immediately), it was forgiving (it resumed cooperation after the opponent did), and clear (its behavior was easy to predict).

Axelrod then went on to apply his insights to evolutionary theory. His models showed that cooperation can arise without central authority, moral preaching, or long-term contracts—simply through repeated, reciprocal interactions among self-interested agents. And his models showed further that a strategy where you open with niceness, coupled with retaliation and forgiveness, was an evolutionarily stable strategy (ESS).

An evolutionarily stable strategy is a strategy that, if adopted by most members of a population, cannot be invaded by a small number of individuals (mutants) using an alternative strategy. And an ESS is also a strategy that does well against copies of itself.

In other words, once an ESS becomes common in a population, natural selection (or imitation of success) will keep it dominant, because any newcomer using a different strategy will do worse, on average, than the ESS.

The big lesson we need to take away from game theory, as we cultivate the sociome with the aim of the betterment of society, is that cooperative positive-sum games in the real world are not just possible, but are in fact commonplace; and that the reason for the success of positive-sum games boils down to individual behavior that is simultaneously competitive and cooperative, and not to top-down interventions.

Governance without governors.

But wait—there's more!

Consider the abundant evidence all around us of the cooperative competition that occurs in the world of sport. In sport, everyone is trying to win (and it would not be much fun to watch or to participate in if it were not so), but they do so within a framework of rules that protect the integrity of the game, rules that are enforced by neutral referees, and that are followed voluntarily by most players most of the time.

Tim Urban, author of the *Wait But Why* blog, argues that this kind of competition—inside and outside of sport—is healthy and productive because it pushes participants to improve, and society as a whole benefits from the resulting excellence, fairness, and clarity.

7

WHAT'S NEXT?

What's next for human society? What will characterize the evolving sociome in both the near and distant future? The short answer is "Nobody knows"; and not only does nobody know, nobody can know.

We are as certain as certain can be that we cannot know, because we have seen a convincing argument that nature is fundamentally unpredictable. This is because so much of the dynamics in natural systems is non-linear, which leads to sensitive dependence on initial conditions, commonly known as the "butterfly effect."

The butterfly effect means that we cannot expect ever to be able to model complex dynamical systems successfully, nor can we expect ever to create reliable forecasts or to exert effective control over outcomes.

We are thus led to the conclusion that we cannot arbitrarily create a lasting societal structure, because in nature structure is secondary, and the societal structures we see around us have been created by processes over which we have only limited control — far more limited than many of us seem to believe.

And that explains why we ought to focus our attention on processes, and not on structures, if we wish to make a contribution to the project of improving the lot of mankind which has a chance of working.

Not only do we need to focus our attention on processes, we need to understand that we cannot intelligently design processes any more than we can intelligently design structures. The processes and the resulting structures have an evolving life of their own, which started long before we were born and will continue long after we die.

Or, another way to put it is that we are obliged to work with sociomes in much the same way we are obliged to work with biomes. We can cultivate an existing biome, and we can cultivate an existing sociome. In neither case can we erase the old one and put a newly constructed one in its place.

Call it what you will — rational mastery, intelligent design, or whatever — it's just not something that is in the cards we have been dealt or ever will be dealt.

So what happens when someone attempts to envision and then create an ideal social structure — utopia, a new deal, national greatness, heaven on earth, etc.?

What happens is the same as what happens whatever we do or whatever we think we are doing. Even if we believe we are designing and creating a society from the ground up, or exerting authority with the aim of keeping things from going off the rails, the efforts we make simply become additional inputs to the energy flows that are *already* operating to organize the sociome. Systems are organized by the energy flowing through them, and not by intelligent design and top-down control.

Evidence continues to mount that political intervention done with *deus ex machina* intentions more often than not creates *diabolus ex machina* results.

So as awareness of the ubiquity of the phenomenon of spontaneous emergent order spreads, fewer and fewer of us will be tempted to propose or to accept intelligent design proposals and ideological crusades where the narrative is that we are living in a society that has been intelligently designed, but by the wrong people, and the only problem we need to solve is how to wrest power from the bad people who currently wield this power and put good people in their place, after which the good people will intelligently design ideal outcomes.

As support for intelligent design solutions and *deus ex machina* intervention wanes, our medievalist institutions will begin to wither away, and they will be replaced by fluid, ever-changing structures that naturally spring up as a result of dynamical processes that will result collectively from our individual efforts.

As we make progress in the cultivation of the sociome, it is likely that the biggest sticking point will be the falconer strategy that has been a feature of politics from time immemorial.

A falconer trains his bird by getting the bird to regard him as the place to go, and the only place to go, for food. After first getting the young bird accustomed to the falconer, the equipment, and the surroundings, the bird learns to attack a lure that the falconer swirls, and when the bird returns the lure to the falconer it gets a reward of food.

Once the bird has been trained with the lure, the falconer turns it loose to hunt for real. The bird brings its kill to the falconer, and the falconer then feeds it — the bird doesn't get it that the falconer is useless from its point of view, since it can get its own food, and the food that it does get from the falconer is something it has killed itself.

The falconer strategy is an analog of what happens in politics. Citizens work and produce, but the state collects taxes and then redistributes benefits to the citizens in the form of benefits, subsidies, or services.

The people, in turn, are encouraged to feel gratitude or loyalty toward those politicians — even though the resources being given back originated with the citizens themselves. People then begin believing that they depend on the government for support, rather than seeing that the government depends on them for its means.

Just as the falcon's dependence gives the falconer leverage, so does redistribution give political power to those who control the flow of benefits.

Control the reward and you control the behavior.

Neither the falcon nor the citizen is "enslaved" outright — they can both, in theory, fly away. But both face the same trade-off, because independence brings risk and uncertainty along with liberty, whereas dependence brings security but also submission.

People forget that the resources redistributed by politicians come from their own collective labor, and they are easily manipulated by the illusion of generosity. The falconer's art depends on maintaining this illusion — that the falcon needs *him* for its meals.

So too, political power can depend on maintaining the illusion that the state creates wealth, rather than merely redistributing it.

If we value freedom, we will resist the blandishments of the politicians offering us "free stuff," or stuff that we will get if we plunder the bank accounts of the rich.

And we will learn to recognize the tried-and-true tactics of moral blackmail and moral intimidation, where we are told that if we do not support government programs to assist the less fortunate, we are morally defective beings.

And if we value prosperity, we have to recognize that the dynamic created in the sociome by diverting people's efforts away from the production of new stuff and toward squabbling over who gets how much of that which has *already* been produced reduces the amount of stuff there will be to go around.

We cannot predict any specifics about the future of the sociome with strong assurance of being right, but I believe we can at least predict an increasing influence of the awareness of natural processes and the acceptance of our place in the natural order as time goes on.

An interesting speculation about the future of our modern sociome is that it might settle into a long-term yin-yang opposition between the ideas and traditions we have inherited from Europe's feudal aristocracy, all based on intelligent design, and the ideas that are based on the revelations of evolutionary processes and emergent order that are attributable to the scientific investigation of nature begun in our modern era by Charles Darwin and carried forward by his intellectual heirs in all areas of study.

Such a state of yin-yang opposition is, in fact, what emerged during the last several thousand years in China as a result of the interactions between the philosophies of Confucianism and Taoism, which on the surface seem to be incompatible, but which have reached a mutual accommodation.

Confucianism, the influence of which was firmly cemented by the civil service exam system begun under the Han Dynasty and then firmly entrenched several centuries later under the Sui and Tang Dynasties, emphasized civic duty, respect for hierarchy, and especially filial piety and traditional family structure as the path to a harmonious and orderly society.

Taoism emphasizes spiritual connection to the natural spontaneous order of the universe and emphasizes simplicity and flexibility. It encourages people to align with nature rather than resist it; to value intuition over rigid rules and humility over ambition. The overriding principle is *wuwei*, or non-action, letting things unfold naturally.

Generation after generation of Chinese have subscribed to both traditions, incompatible though they seem, by adopting a dual lifestyle — honoring Confucian principles during the daytime as a path to social order, for example, and honoring Taoist principles after hours as a path to personal fulfillment and spiritual development.

The parallels between ancient Confucianism in China and medievalist intelligent design thinking in Europe, and between Taoism and modern evolutionary thinking, are striking.

It is said that history does not repeat itself, but that it does rhyme. The course of the synthesis between the conflicting ideas derived from intelligent design thinking and the ideas derived from evolutionary thinking might very well rhyme with the synthesis that evolved between Confucianism and Taoism; or our societies could find a novel course, a new way forward.

I personally believe that an increasing awareness of the pervasiveness of self-organizing systems in the natural world, of which we are a part, along with a deepening understanding of the way of nature based on scientific investigation, will lead to far less reliance on the institution of government, as we learn that we can have an orderly and just sociome with far less giving or taking of orders.

And I believe further that we can profitably use one particular feature of evolved human behavior, and that feature is an almost universal moral intuition, which includes at least lip service to, and often an extensive observance of, the golden rule. If you search you will find mention of the golden rule all over the planet and throughout history.

Our evolved moral intuition also generally includes, as a corollary, a condemnation of stealing, or, to put it another way, the observance of property rights.

We can use both of these facets of our evolved moral intuition to help us and the people we interact with to live our daily lives so as to form networks of competitive cooperation and networks of mutual care, with far less of those in a position of authority giving us orders or taking our stuff.

Better governance, fewer governors.

ABOUT THE AUTHOR

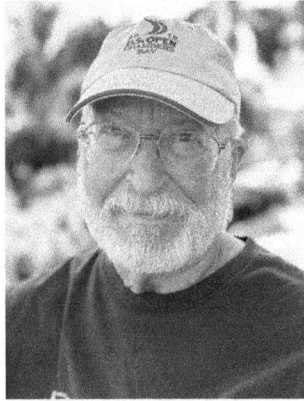

Eric Moon is a writer, educator, and systems thinker whose work explores how complex order arises naturally in human society.

He originally studied history at the University of Washington, completing three years before shifting his focus to economics—a transition that deepened his interest in how human systems evolve over time. Drawing from decades of study, Eric bridges disciplines to reveal how spontaneous processes—not design—shape our social world.

His podcast, *Fascinating!*, has reached thousands of listeners worldwide, sparking a growing movement toward understanding "governance without governors."